WRITERS AND THEIR WORK: NO 110

Thackeray

by

LAURENCE BRANDER

Published for the British Council
by Longman Group Ltd

Forty New Pence net

W. M. Thackeray (1811-1863), who was born in Calcutta, came from a prosperous family, many of whose members had served in India. After leading a dilettante life, as a young man, in London and in Paris, Thackeray married, lost his considerable fortune and settled down to write for a living. Later, his private happiness was shattered when his wife became insane and was obliged to live apart from him in the care of an attendant. Thereafter he devoted himself to the profession of letters, and to the welfare of his two surviving daughters.

Thackeray wrote satirical short novels and full-scale panoramic works of fiction; he was an accomplished writer of light verse and a skilful lecturer; as editor of the *Cornhill* he had a popular platform for his occasional essays and lay sermons.

Mr Brander argues that *Vanity Fair* is Thackeray's masterpiece, a novel in which all his gifts are fused in a unique creative glow and fire. The Pendennis novels are 'the greatest panorama of London life ever offered in a novel sequence' and an incomparable portrait of England in the 1850's.

Mr Brander's publications include critical studies of E. M. Forster, Aldous Huxley and George Orwell. He is also the author of two essays in the present series, *Smollett* (No. 11) and *Hood* (No. 159).

¶ WILLIAM MAKEPEACE THACKERAY was born in Calcutta on 18 July 1811. He died in London on 24 December 1863.

THACKERAY

from the portrait by SAMUEL LAURENCE
National Portrait Gallery

THACKERAY

by

LAURENCE BRANDER

PUBLISHED FOR
THE BRITISH COUNCIL
BY LONGMAN GROUP LTD

LONGMAN GROUP LTD
Longman House, Burnt Mill, Harlow, Essex

*Associated companies, branches and
representatives throughout the world*

First published 1959
Revised edition 1964
Reprinted with minor amendments and additions to Bibliography 1970
© Laurence Brander 1959, 1964

*Printed in Great Britain by
F. Mildner & Sons, London, EC1*

THACKERAY

I. INTRODUCTION

WHEN the nineteenth century opened, the population of London was less than a million. By 1861, in Thackeray's last years, it was growing rapidly towards three millions. At the beginning of the century, immense docks were being built in the Thames estuary and new bridges were being thrown across the river. In the 'thirties and 'forties the railways came to London and the age of the post-chaise which Dickens loved to celebrate had come to an end.

The towns and villages which clustered round Westminster and the City became one unending sprawl, and the boroughs which then formed London were the greatest agglomeration of humanity ever known in the western world. All these people had to be entertained, and the provision of home entertainment became an industry, for there was plenty of middle class money about. It was an industry in which publishers especially interested themselves, and the age of Dickens and Thackeray became the age of reading. It was the age of the magazine and the monthly part, it was the age of the travel book and the first age of the reprinting of English classics. The average yearly number of new books rose from 850 between 1802 and 1807 to about 2,530 in 1853.

Everyone except the most serious-minded read novels. Scott had made the novel respectable. It offered entertainment and a pattern of living. A wonderful market was open to Dickens and Thackeray with the result that *Dombey and Son* and *Vanity Fair* were on sale at the same time in shilling parts. Dickens created a world of his own; a world essentially London which yet had never quite existed. Thackeray offered to his own Kensington and the new boroughs a picture of upper middle-class life in the ancient boroughs. In his own time they said he was a realist. Just after his death Bagehot wrote: 'A painfulness certainly clings like an atmosphere round Mr Thackeray's writings, in consequence of his inseparable and ever-present realism.'

Thackeray drew a picture of the life and struggles of the rich and powerful middle class. He filled his books with the people of Bloomsbury and Mayfair and Kensington. He described their lives and their ideals so that they could enjoy the mirror, and so that suburbia could imitate them; and he did it because all his readers preferred that to anything else he offered them. Even while he was still producing the Pendennis novels, Bagehot wrote of Thackeray's suburban public: 'The delicate touches of our great satirist have, for such readers, not only the charm of wit, but likewise the interest of valuable information; he tells them of the topics which they want to know.'

Thackeray has many pleasures to offer. He can tell a story, *Barry Lyndon* and *Esmond*. He can make characters; no other English novelist more quickly and easily except Dickens; and Thackeray supplements the Dickens world with characters Dickens could never have drawn. Dickens could never have given us a mature man like Colonel Lambert, or a sophisticated one like Major Pendennis. Dickens's characters had quite remarkably undeveloped minds. For the same reason, Dickens could never have given us Becky or Beatrix or that most wonderful young woman, Ethel Newcome. The special pleasure Thackeray offers is that he can write. Again, so can Dickens. But not every English novelist writes well, and Thackeray could manage this difficult language, English, with most enviable skill.

He exercised his skill in two ways. He has a narrative style of weight and pace, best enjoyed in *Barry Lyndon*, *Vanity Fair* and *Esmond*, and developed in a special way in *The Virginians*. In *Denis Duval*, at the end, he uses a narrative style that is much more modern. The other style, which he used in the Pendennis series, was informal, conversational, diffuse. This was Thackeray himself; this, so far as technique is concerned, was his unique excellence. His early writing is good, well-paced narrative, with the ostentatious energy of

Regency life. His writing in the golden decade, the 'fifties of last century, and just beyond it, is superb. Its secret was an easy yet disciplined colloquialism which makes it impossible to misread him when reading aloud. And reading aloud was a favourite Victorian pastime.

He could write and he was always writing. He had an endless gusto of creative energy. From the moment he lost his money as a young man, he wrote, and he never stopped writing till he died. 'As soon as a piece of work is out of hand', he wrote in a late *Roundabout* paper, 'and before going to sleep, I like to begin another; it may be to write only half a dozen lines: but that is something towards Number the Next.'

II.   THE LIFE

Thackeray's life was the material out of which the Pendennis books, and much before them, was made. He was born in Calcutta in 1811 and was brought home in 1816. He never returned to India, so his knowledge of India and the Anglo-Indian society of his time came from observing his family and their connections. The dear old military men, for example, who had served in the East India Company's army came from his step-father and his friends. Thackeray's father was a senior civilian in the Company's service, and we can best glimpse him in a Chinnery drawing of the Thackeray family when William was three. Richmond Thackeray, the father, died in 1815 and the child was sent home to school in the following year.

His mother stayed on in Calcutta to marry again, and for the moment the focus must be on her. For what happened to her when she was a teen-ager made so strong an impression on Thackeray that it supplied one of the themes which gave most energy to his satire in the great novels. It was the theme of the marriage market and the conduct of parents when finding husbands for their daughters.

As a girl, Thackeray's mother had fallen in love with a young officer, Captain Carmichael-Smyth. Her parents disapproved, and when he had to go away they intercepted his letters to her and lied to both of them. She was told he had died, and he was told that she no longer wished to hear from him. She was sent out to Calcutta where she married Richmond Thackeray. One evening Richmond Thackeray came home and told his wife there would be an additional guest to dinner. He had met a most amusing officer down from Agra and had invited him. The unexpected guest arrived. It was Carmichael-Smyth. The shock was terrible for both of them. After dinner they contrived to talk privately and they realized how they had been duped. The young officer returned forthwith to Agra. Eighteen months after her husband's death, Mrs Thackeray married her first lover.

Meantime, Thackeray was unwillingly at school. When he left his first school and went to Charterhouse he still did not enjoy himself. Time and Cambridge eventually cured that unhappiness, and after Cambridge he made various false and rather dilettante attempts at finding a profession. The truth was that his father had left him too much money. He thought of art and of the law. He went to Paris to study art. There he fell in love, and as he lost his money at the same time, his fond step-father had to find a means of providing for him. He ingeniously bought a newspaper so that Thackeray could be appointed Paris correspondent and marry. The newspaper did not take long to fail, and then Thackeray found in his mother-in-law's behaviour a model for the Campaigner and Mrs Baynes.

Soon the young couple were living in Bloomsbury, like the young people in *The Great Hoggarty Diamond* and in *Philip*. Children came, three daughters, of whom one died as a baby, and after the third was born, calamity. Mrs Thackeray lost her reason and had to live with an attendant in the country. She outlived Thackeray, so he was condemned to a widower's life for ever. He had one sentimental friendship sufficiently deep to disturb him seriously, with Mrs Brookfield. That story, with its abrupt termination, has now been fully told. Afterwards, as the two girls grew older, his life centred more and more on them.

A writer's domestic life is likely to be as simple as the life of the Vicar of Wakefield, who moved from the blue bed to the brown but never any farther. Thackeray moved from Bloomsbury to Kensington, where finally he built himself the lovely house in Palace Gardens which is now the Israeli Embassy. His life can be followed in the many portraits, drawings and photographs that were made of him, and the pictures and photographs of the rooms in which he wrote. He was a great friend of many artists, and was happy to live publicly in this way. By contrast, the intense privacy of a writer's life is seen in the *Roundabout Papers*, where the writer sits remembering and reflecting on paper. These papers are amongst the best autobiographical writing in the language and amongst the most revealing glimpses of the Victorian mind.

It was a good life, spent in energetic creation. He loved writing and he was always writing. He loved drawing and he was always drawing. He had an endless zest for creation and he came to his full fame and powers in the most glorious decade London has ever known, the 'fifties of last century. No great man in that society was a lonely eminence. Everyone of stature was surrounded by his peers. They lived to the full, hospitably and convivially. By the nature of his domestic loneliness, Thackeray depended more than most men on society. He spent his life in that ebullient society and in describing it.

After his death, Bagehot assessed Thackeray's contribution with his usual perceptiveness. Trollope, a little later, celebrated him sensibly and solidly in the English Men of Letters series. That book occasionally turns up in the second-hand bookshops and is well worth reading. The next notable assessment was by Saintsbury in his Introductions to the Oxford edition, which is especially useful in giving

Thackeray's original and revised readings. Meanwhile, Gissing had introduced an effective comparison with Dickens in his book on Dickens; and a little later than all this, Chesterton produced a masterly short essay. All these tributes are by London bookmen on a great London bookman.

Contemporary work speaks for itself, but anyone writing on Thackeray will wish to acknowledge indebtedness to Professor Gordon Ray, whose sensible and sensitive devotion to Thackeray's work has produced all that the student can desire.

III. THE EARLY WORK AND *BARRY LYNDON*

For all his early works Thackeray used that popular medium the magazine. One or two of the journalists whom Thackeray met in his early newspaper days were, in the 'thirties, working for *Fraser's Magazine*. Mr Fraser of Regent Street followed the fashion of the time in offering a monthly collection of stories, essays and travel pieces. There was much Improvement in the mixture, for Mr Fraser had a Scottish tact in catering for his public. The earliest numbers were devoted to decorum, dullness, and the usual list of bankrupts. But the Magazine survived, and eventually Thackeray was employed to offer light relief, which he began to do in the *Yellowplush* papers in 1837-8. In the first year of Queen Victoria's reign the public taste, it would appear, was for robust, simple fun and Thackeray spiced his with a wit that darts, and strikes more than one target. Yellowplush in this sample is addressing his fellow-servants in their club just after thay have discovered he is an author:

'I am', says I, in a neat spitch, 'I am a littery man—there is no shame in it in the present instins; though, in general, its a blaggard employment enough. But it aint my *trade*—it isnt for the looker of gain that I sitt pen to payper—it is in the saycred caws of nollitch.' (*Hear, hear.*)

Equally extravagant, with a farcical extravagance which was for some time to be Thackeray's favourite Irish manner, was *Major Gahagan*, which appeared in the following year in the *New Monthly Magazine*, still edited by Theodore Hook. The literature of extravagance in English is delightful, and there is much amusement in this example. Major Gahagan has discovered that his beloved in the besieged town has none of her favourite elephant steak for supper. But outside lie the elephants the Major killed only a couple of days ago:

I rushed out; not a single man would follow. The bodies of the elephants we had killed still lay on the ground where they had fallen, about four hundred yards from the fort. I descended calmly the hill, a very steep one, and coming to the spot, took my pick of the animals, choosing a tolerably small and plump one, of about thirteen feet high, which the vultures had respected. I threw this animal over my shoulders, and made for the fort.

As I marched up the declivity, whizz—piff—whirr! came the balls over my head; and pitter-patter, pitter-patter they fell on the body of the elephant like drops of rain. The enemy were behind me; I knew it, and quickened my pace. I heard the gallop of their horse: they came nearer, nearer; I was within a hundred yards of the fort—seventy—fifty! I strained every nerve; I panted with superhuman exertion—I ran—could a man run very fast with such a tremendous weight on his shoulders?

Alas, the Major's efforts to provide a steak for his beloved's supper are made at the expense of his own safety. He drops in a faint as he shoves the elephant through the gate of the citadel: 'exhausted nature could bear no more.'

In the following year, 1839, *Catherine* appeared in *Fraser's*. It had the same energy of invention, in a very different mood, for it pretended to be a most serious exposure of crime stories popular at that time, and was in fact itself a very good one. It was the first of Thackeray's short novels, a kind in which he became expert. The story line was usually melodramatic, rising to a final scene when all the principal characters appear. *Catherine* was based on a particularly atrocious murder, which offered Thackeray a gruesome finale.

The opening however is a village scene, soldiers and rustics on the village green, and for the first time Thackeray sketches rural England, as he was to do so often and so memorably. For the first time there is a plot, comparatively real characters, and a background that is perfectly real. The prose takes on colour and pace; the *tempo* of the story rises.

The technique is repeated a year later in *Fraser's* in *A Shabby Genteel Story*. The characters move and speak in the jerky way puppets have, but there is story interest, with a Cinderella heroine and a bogus young artist who is carried off in the end by a rich old woman who marries him. The prose is simple and speedy and that, like the youthfully hard story line, contrasts sharply with the note which Thackeray appended at the end of the 1857 reprint in his *Miscellanies:*

> When the republication of these Miscellanies was announced, it was my intention to complete the little story, of which only the first part is here written. Perhaps novel-readers will understand, even from the above chapters, what was to ensue. . . . The tale was interrupted at a sad period of the writer's own life. The colours are long since dry; the artist's hand is changed.

Between the writing of the story and the note, the Victorian Age had arrived.

In the next story, in the following year, there were affinities with his later work. In fact, *The Great Hoggarty Diamond* is in many ways an early version of the halcyon story in *Philip* of young married life in Bloomsbury. In its main theme, the rise and fall of Mr Brough, the swindling financier, it is as harsh as any of the early short novels. It foreshadows a notable aspect of the Pendennis stories in having an overbearing female clouding and harassing the lives of the young people. An Irish aunt lives with them and on them, and generally deprives them of happiness. The dominant note is a welcome one, for it is a lyrical description of young married life, which is an autobiographical celebration. The whole business of learning to live, dealing with servants, entertaining, meeting the bills, these and the aura of happiness. In these pleasantly sentimental realistic descriptions Thackeray was never surpassed and here, in *The Great Hoggarty Diamond*, they first appear.

The most agreeable way to return to these early stories is by reading them in the four volumes of the *Miscellanies* which Thackeray himself collected in 1857, which were so often reprinted and which are still fairly easy to obtain. These volumes contain much more material than there has been room to discuss here, and most of it is still amusing to anyone who enjoys the harsh, male Regency spirit as well as the first buds of Victorian sentiment. There are readers who prefer these early stories to anything Thackeray wrote later, and certainly there are many who prefer them to the Thackeray of the Pendennis sequence, with its diffuse manner and its regular interruptions by the narrator as commentator and moralist.

Most of these early pieces are vigorous story-telling on the simple formula of having a beginning which quickly leads to a middle which hurries to a full-stage ending. They are full of villains, because villains are full of energy—and often generosity—which makes for good story-telling; not at all because villains can be preached about. In these early stories there is no preaching. They are simple, elementary narratives, sophisticated pleasantly with touches of satire:

> Yes, thank Heaven! there is about a freeborn Briton a cringing baseness and lick-spittle awe of rank, which does not exist under any tyranny in Europe, and is only to be found here and in America.

There are two more items in this collection of early material which must be noticed. First, *The Book of Snobs*, which appeared in *Punch* in 1846-7. Thackeray had been warned not to touch *Punch* when it first appeared in 1841. The warning was reasonable, and *Punch* failed to excite the market until Hood's *Song of a Shirt* appeared in the Christmas Number of 1843.

Thackeray ignored the advice. The *Snob* papers are the best of his contributions to *Punch*, and it is fair to say that

along with Jerrold's *Mrs Caudle's Curtain Lectures*, which
appeared at the same time, they gave *Punch* the vitality
which set it on its long career. One way of enjoying the
Snob papers is to contrast them with *Boz*. In *Boz*, Dickens
exploited very early his genius for describing a place and
making it real and stereoscopic in our mind's eye. In the
Snob, Thackeray exploited very early his satirical genius for
bringing a character alive in a sentence and giving him
identity in a page. The *Snob* papers are, most of them,
brilliant sketches of London types, and can be enjoyed today
because the same sort of people are going about awaiting
the same critical attention.

The other item which must be noticed is the most
important piece in the collection, *Barry Lyndon*, his first
full-length novel. *Barry Lyndon* is well organized, and for
those who like Thackeray the story-teller rather than
Thackeray the diffuse creator of a society, it stands between
the shorter novels and *Esmond*. Like them, it is taut story-
telling. Indeed, apart from the last chapters, which tell the
unbearable story of how Barry treated his wife and step-son,
it is uncommonly good story-telling. All the hints and
suggestions contained in the sketches and the shorter novels
are fused for the first time into a coherent point of view.
Barry Lyndon is the last of his Regency pieces, though written
in the next reign. Like the others, it would seem to be based
on ridicule. But here, his characters are not ridiculous. They
are noticeable figures in the European scene, and in all his
work afterwards Thackeray was ready not only to reach
back into the eighteenth century but to reach across to
Western Europe. His great panoramas needed space as well
as time; and it would seem that here he accepted the world
as a Vanity Fair in which evil was the active, dominating
spirit, and selfishness was the driving energy of the world.

Barry Lyndon was the last piece Thackeray published in
magazine form until he contributed *Lovel the Widower* to
his own *Cornhill* in 1860. In the next decade, the 'fifties, he
wrote another series of shorter pieces which appeared in a

new publishing format, the Christmas Book. The Christmas Book replaced the Annual, which had been in favour during the 'thirties. Hood had extended the range of the Annuals in his famous Comic Annuals, and it was this tradition of Christmas gaiety which the publisher now exploited. Far and away the most famous of them is Dickens's *Christmas Carol*, and probably the only other Christmas Book popularly remembered is Thackeray's *Rose and the Ring*. But Thackeray produced them regularly for some years, and we may couple them with his verses to illustrate the abundant fecundity of his genius.

Like many good prosemen, Thackeray, when he wrote verse, wrote light verse. When he wanted to express himself, he used prose. When he wanted to be gay, he might use prose or verse or make little drawings. Some of his verses, like 'Little Bill-ee', have become part of the delightful furniture of the English nursery mind. Otherwise, they have been forgotten.

So has another piece which once found favour. We live in an age when travel books are a favourite form of publishing and travel books of all times are enjoyed. But Thackeray's *Cornhill to Cairo* is almost and rightly forgotten. Like the Christmas books, it was in response to a popular publishing kind. Like them, it appeared in an attractive format, expensively illustrated. Only the strongest appetite for travel books can make it readable today.

IV. *VANITY FAIR*

There was another kind of publishing, which Dickens had used with great success, and which Thackeray, perhaps for that very reason, had not attempted. It was the fashion of producing a novel in shilling monthly parts. Thackeray used it at last for *Vanity Fair*, and as these monthly parts appeared, Thackeray, who already enjoyed a considerable though not an outstanding reputation as a writer, suddenly found himself famous.

It is his greatest work. Nothing before it is in anything like the same class in sweep and energy. After it came the Pendennis sequence and *Esmond*, but none of them challenge the creative glow and richness of *Vanity Fair*. It was as sudden as it was unrepeatable, and though Thackeray explored back through time a hundred years, and exploited all the resources of his experience and personality, he never managed anything so powerful again.

The story moves steadily, even speedily, right from the start; and it was getting a story under way that Thackeray so often found difficult. The characters come alive at once, and they are all easy to meet. The prose is richly warm, well paced narrative. Salty too, for it carries neater, harder comments than anywhere else. Ridicule has given way to irony. The whole performance has brilliance and power so well under control that none of it is wasted.

He gathers into this novel all his special skills. All his life he wrote about London for Londoners and anyone else who cared to listen. He never wrote about it better than in this broad panorama. He was a maker of characters, and he never made characters more vividly real than he did here. He was an historical novelist, and nowhere else has he given so poignantly the sense of the moral desolation of war, which makes so much of human history. He painted portraits of London families, and the Osbornes and the Sedleys are amongst his most finished family portraits; they are certainly so in illustrating his private theme that the family and the household could conceal great cruelty, which can never be discovered and for which there is no redress.

It is one of the few novels in which Thackeray is Olympian. In *Barry Lyndon* he is tough and satirical. In *Esmond* he becomes a great English aristocrat of the eighteenth century. In the Pendennis sequence he is a great contemporary personality to his first readers. But in *Vanity Fair* he has an Olympian impersonality, with only an occasional personal intrusion to sharpen the focus. Much later, in *The Virginians*, he does the same, at a critical point dropping the impersonal omniscience to tell the story personally and give the needed warmth of feeling.

Being an historical panorama, *Vanity Fair* had to be given shape and proportion. So it was written as a book, like *Esmond*, and not as a narrative stream, like the Pendennis books. Like all successful long novels, it is a series of scenes which follow one another not accidentally but as calculated contrasts, high life alternating with low, the tension of pain with the relaxation of comedy.

The scenes build up into the panorama effect which is secured by withdrawing the point of observation so that the focus broadens to take in the European scene at the time of Waterloo. Thackeray later gets a similar effect in *The Virginians*, when he is celebrating the youth of a people on a vast land mass. He is more certain in the earlier focus of *Vanity Fair*, and that certainty is, as always, a matter of time as well as space. He is writing of a time which his older friends had known and out of which he himself grew. The atmosphere of it was his birthright.

It is always so with the historical novelist; collective memory is truer than the greatest imaginative conception of earlier times. So *Vanity Fair* is more true than *Esmond* and *The Virginians*. It is not more true than the Pendennis novels, but it has this advantage, that its point in space-time gives it a unity and finality which the other great panoramic compositions cannot have because they merge into the present.

Among the characters the women are the most interesting, and the contrast between Becky and Amelia is one of the most discussed subjects in English fiction. In a sense, Amelia is the stronger woman. Once or twice she becomes uncontrollably angry and at once gets what she wants. Becky, we notice, can fail in a crisis. She cannot prevent Rawdon from knocking Steyne down. On one occasion she gives way to selfless generosity, when she surprises Amelia out of her dreams and shows her how wrong she was to idolize the memory of George, how cruelly selfish she was being to Dobbin.

There was a moment, when Dobbin first returned from Madras, at which all could have gone well. It was his meeting with Amelia in Kensington Gardens:

He looked at her—oh, how fondly—as she came running towards him, her hands before her, ready to give them to him. She wasn't changed. She was a little pale: a little stouter in figure. Her eyes were the same, the kind trustful eyes. There were scarce three lines of silver in her soft brown hair. She gave him both her hands as she looked up flushing and smiling through her tears into his honest homely face. He took the two little hands between his two, and held them there. He was speechless for a moment. Why did he not take her in his arms, and swear that he would never leave her? She must have yielded: she could not but have obeyed him.

'I—I've another arrival to announce', he said, after a pause.

'Mrs Dobbin?' Amelia said, making a movement back—Why didn't he speak?

'No', he said, letting her hands go: 'Who has told you those lies?—I mean, your brother Jos came in the same ship with me, and is come home to make you all happy.'

The moment passed, and much happened before Becky, in a moment of good sense and generosity, settled the question. She is speaking to Amelia:

'... You are no more fit to live in the world than a baby in arms. You must marry, or you and your precious boy will go to ruin. You must have a husband, you fool; and one of the best gentlemen I ever saw has offered you a hundred times, and you have rejected him, you silly, heartless, ungrateful little creature!'

'I tried—I tried my best, indeed I did, Rebecca', said Amelia, deprecatingly, 'but I couldn't forget . . .' and she finished the sentence by looking up at the portrait.

'Couldn't forget *him*!' cried out Becky, 'that selfish humbug, that low-bred cockney dandy, that padded booby, who had neither wit, nor manners, nor heart, and was no more to be compared to your friend with the bamboo cane, than you are to Queen Elizabeth. Why, the man was weary of you, and would have jilted you, but that Dobbin forced him to keep his word. He owned it to me. He never cared for you. He used to sneer about you to me, time after time; and made love to me the week after he married you.'

'It's false! It's false! Rebecca', cried Amelia, starting up.

'Look there, you fool', Becky said, still with provoking good humour, and taking a little paper out of her belt, she opened it and flung it into Emmy's lap. 'You know his handwriting. He wrote that to me— wanted me to run away with him—gave it me under your nose, the day before he was shot—and served him right!' Becky repeated.

Emmy did not hear her; she was looking at the letter. It was that which George had put into the bouquet and given to Becky on the night of the Duchess of Richmond's ball. It was as she said: the foolish young man had asked her to fly.

That is shock treatment of dramatic quality[1] and the woman who gives it is the outstanding character in the book. She is the most remarkable character in Thackeray's long series of female portraits. She is eternally energetic and always scheming. She is provocative, inspiring and dangerous as fire. Beatrix Esmond alone can stand beside her, and even Beatrix only rivals her by possessing the tragic quality of the mistress who is fatal to the men she loves.

The emotional pitch in *Vanity Fair* is higher throughout than in any other Thackeray novel. It is only rivalled in the great *Esmond* scenes, as when Esmond returns from the wars to Lady Castlewood and Beatrix at Winchester. The prose is taut, as always in the pastiche of *Esmond*, and as in the great historical passages in *The Virginians*. All this combines to give *Vanity Fair* a richness of texture and a wealth of energy and colour which makes it a panoramic display without a rival in English fiction.

[1] But see Mrs Tillotson in *Novels of the Eighteen-Forties*, p. 244. 'Amelia has already relented and written to recall Dobbin. The inner necessity of the scene is rather to leave no sham unexposed.' It is also possible that but for Becky's candour Amelia might have hesitated at the last moment again.

V. *ESMOND* AND *THE VIRGINIANS*

Vanity Fair opened up for Thackeray two lines of development. He could exploit his gift for painting the London scene; he could write historical novels. He did both. His next novel was *Pendennis;* and in that sequence, as it became, *The Newcomes* and *Philip* followed over a decade. After *Pendennis* he wrote *Esmond*, followed by *The Virginians*. In this, towards the end, there is a reference to Barry Lyndon, and the Warringtons make a link with *Pendennis*. By means of such links throughout his work, Thackeray built up a whole society.

Among the advantages of writing about former times, Thackeray exploited two. First, the composition has the completeness of a story of long ago, with everything finished and the values of the actions all decided. Second, real people of some fame in the world are introduced. Such characters are best on the fringe, and Thackeray in *Esmond* satisfies his dislike and contempt for Marlborough by showing his influence while hardly ever bringing him on the scene. In the same way, his view that the Stuarts were quite unequal to their opportunities of regaining their throne, and unworthy of their followers, can be best expressed by keeping the Pretender off stage as much as possible, though he is at the centre of a crisis late in the story. Both Marlborough and the Pretender are influences, great influences suitable to their rank, rather than characters.

The characters are the lesser aristocracy, of a rank and station high enough to give Thackeray a chance to develop tragic situations, but not so high that their actions and characters are so well known that they hamper his creative freedom.

The development of Beatrix in all her beauty and fatality is one of the great glories of English fiction. As a young girl, her irresponsible prattle leads to her father's death. As a woman, her actions lead to the death of the Duke she was going to marry. It is a portrait of an irresistibly beautiful

woman who was cursed with a flaw in her nature which was
fatal and unchangeable.

Her mother is in complete contrast, a mother type. In
the beginning, she is like a mother to Esmond. Half-way
through, when he makes a young man's profession of love
to her, she insists on the mother relationship. At the end,
when he has matured, and the few years between them have
become as nothing, they marry. Meantime, between his first
declaration and their confession of love and their marriage,
Esmond is at the mercy of the beauty and cruelty of Beatrix.

Like the two women in *Vanity Fair*, these two are much
more real than any of the men in the book. The story
proceeds in its astonishing pastiche of eighteenth-century
prose through the story of Castlewood and Mohun to the
campaigns of Marlborough, and through an imaginary and
abortive visit of the Pretender to London. The scene widens,
as the boy Esmond grows into manhood, from the English
countryside to London and to Europe.

The story is beautifully managed. The characters develop
and live in the context of great events and everything that
happens seems inevitable. The scenes in the great country
house at the beginning, tinged with the sadness of remem-
brance of times long past and places far away; then the
London scenes in Thackeray's Kensington, but a hundred
and fifty years earlier; the battle pieces in Flanders and
Esmond's return to find Beatrix grown and beautiful:

Esmond had left a child and found a woman, grown beyond the
common height; and arrived at such a dazzling completeness of beauty,
that his eyes might well show surprise and delight at beholding her. In
hers there was a brightness so lustrous and melting, that I have seen a
whole assembly follow her as if by an attraction irresistible: and that
night the great Duke was at the playhouse after Ramillies, every soul
turned and looked (she chanced to enter at the opposite side of the theatre
at the same moment) at her, and not at him. She was a brown beauty:
that is, her eyes, hair, and eyebrows and eyelashes were dark: her hair
curling with rich undulations, and waving over her shoulders; but her
complexion was as dazzling white as snow in sunshine: except her

cheeks, which were bright red, and her lips, which were of a still deeper crimson. Her mouth and chin, they said, were too large and full, and so they might be for a goddess in marble, but not for a woman whose eyes were fire, whose look was love, whose voice was the sweetest low song, whose shape was perfect symmetry, health, decision, activity, whose foot as it planted itself on the ground was firm but flexible, and whose motion, whether rapid or slow, was always perfect grace—agile as a nymph, lofty as a queen—now melting, now imperious, now sarcastic—there was no single movement of hers but was beautiful. As he thinks of her, he who writes feels young again, and remembers a paragon.

This is the excitement and sentiment of Steele, and when Thackeray quotes one of his *Spectator* papers the texture of the prose does not change. To complete the eighteenth-century illusion, Thackeray had the early editions printed with the long eighteenth-century 's'. But the book was not popular. The public preferred the present they did not know to the past for which they cared nothing. Thackeray returned to his Pendennis stories, and when he did write a sequel to *Esmond* in *The Virginians* he seems to be thinking of his public in America.

In our remoter calculation there would seem to be one serious flaw in the book. Thackeray chooses to tell the story through a narrator who is at the centre of the story, and who is interested. In most ways that helps, because the central character, through whom we see these great events, is equal to describing and judging them. He can form a judgement on Marlborough and the Pretender as easily as on Dick Steele or his servant, John Lockwood.

All this gives the hero, the narrator, status. But he is interested. He takes sides. In the great historical judgements in the book, on Marlborough and on the Pretender, he is biased. The bias may have been Thackeray's. But if we compare this version of the conflict between Stuarts and Hanoverians with the version in Scott's *Waverley*, we see at once the advantage Scott enjoys by being the Olympian narrator. He can see the virtues on both sides. Vich Ian Vohr and Colonel Talbot are both heroic. Both command our

admiration. The tragedy of the conflict is therefore heigh-
tened. The flaw in Esmond is that the Stuart Pretender never
catches our sympathy, and never seems worth the trouble
his followers took about him.

There is a contrasting atmosphere in the sequel, *The
Virginians*. The atmosphere of *Esmond* is the English country
house and the village attached to it, the neat little houses of
eighteenth-century London and the Low Countries in rather
stuffy weather. The atmosphere of *The Virginians* is the vast
free air of America, with for contrast the cramped quarters of
an almost *papier mâché* Tunbridge Wells.

The Virginians is a vast attempt. It describes the breaking
away of a young nation from the parent. His generous
picture of the young American people, with all the freshness
of their honour and their seriousness about them, makes us
sympathize with them and not with England. The Americans
are given all that Thackeray thought became a man, the
English all that is foolish and weak in the conduct of war and
affairs of state. This he could be sure would be enjoyed by
readers on both sides of the Atlantic. Yet *The Virginians* fails
to be real and convincing. It lacks the chemistry which turns
make-believe into reality, that reality in a novel which is
more intense than the run of our ordinary lives.

Thackeray in later life wanted to become an historian, to
emulate Hume and Smollett and rival his contemporary
Macaulay. When he felt that his creative power was leaving
him, the art of the historian would exercise his critical talent
and that sensitive instrument his prose. *The Virginians* lies
half way between *Vanity Fair* and the histories he never
lived to write. For the finest thing in *The Virginians* is the
sweep and strength of the historical opening.

When he died, he was writing *Denis Duval*, a fascinating
fragment. His creative faculty has revived. His story-telling
power has returned, but his prose is modified. Instead of
depending markedly upon an eighteenth-century base, it is
so modern it reminds us of the best of Stevenson. The setting
is Winchelsea and Rye, and these ancient Channel towns are

recreated for us in a mood which almost recalls Thomas Hardy. So in his last piece, Thackeray is moving towards the next generation of story-tellers.

The fragment appeared in *Cornhill* in 1864, posthumously. It did credit to his memory. There is no longer, as in the early stories, that passionate desire to write of evil which is a characteristic of the story-teller fixed forever in immaturity. The story-teller in *Denis Duval* is in the second part of life, when the strands which hold society together are seen to be weak, and to need any strengthening that can be given. 'Virtue coheres, vice separates' is the theme which Dr Bernard proposes again and again in this story, which in its unpretentious simplicity carries us back to the time before all the great novels, when Thackeray was providing regular amusement in the magazines.

VI. THE PENDENNIS SEQUENCE

One of the most obvious things about the Pendennis novels is Thackeray's refusal to use the tension of suspense. In *Philip*, for example, to make quite sure of this at one point he says:

I do not seek to create even surprises in this modest history, or condescend to keep candid readers in suspense about many matters which might possibly interest them. For instance, the matter of love has interested novel-readers for hundreds of years past, and doubtless will continue so to interest them. ... Phil's first love affair, to which we are now coming, was a false start. I own it at once.

The marked quality of the Pendennis sequence is diffuseness. The reader is attracted by the writing, which is to say by the character of the narrator; and that character is what every novelist depends on in the end. The effect is panoramic, as in *Vanity Fair*, not as in that piece by calculated construction, but by a continuing sprawl of scenes and characters which are held together and become organic only by the loosest mechanism.

The abrupt changes of scene and the introduction of whole series of new characters were possible in the monthly part system, and how much Thackeray relied on that it is not possible to guess. The point is that he permitted himself to do so and produced triumphantly an imaginative world.

The narrator grows up in *Pendennis* and tells the story in *The Newcomes* and *Philip*. He is obviously a man in his forties and fifties, sympathetically looking back at his own youth, and just as sympathetically looking at young Clive Newcome and Philip. He is a charming Victorian gentleman of moderate means, happily married and almost uxorious, with his whole life based on his family and his writing. He is Thackeray himself, plus what Thackeray would have liked for himself. To some of us in London today, he might be the image of one of our friends.

In the Introduction to *Pendennis*, which he wrote after the book was finished, Thackeray speaks of the novel as a 'sort of confidential talk'. This is an exact description of the sequence. For the method is an extension of the essay method, an essayist projecting this world through his personality.

It is an immensely rich world. It is still the greatest panorama of London life ever offered in a classic novel sequence. It embraces the world as upper-class Londoners then enjoyed it, from Kensington Gardens to Brighton, from Baden to Rome. Thackeray was the sharp realist, and the Pendennis world is a true picture of the world out of which London now has grown. Bagehot expresses it well: 'The visible scene of life—the streets, the servants, the clubs, the gossip, the West End—fastened on his brain. These were to him reality. They burnt in upon his brain; they pained his nerves; their influence reached him through many avenues, which ordinary men do not feel much, or to which they are altogether impervious. He had distinct and rather painful sensations where most men have but confused and blurred ones.'

Pendennis is written on the Apprenticeship[1] pattern, a Romantic pattern which gives the story of the writer's own growth. In Dickens, *David Copperfield*. In some ways Thackeray used the pattern better in *Philip*, for Philip himself is drawn with more psychological depth and he is more real and likeable than Pendennis. On the other hand, it is a kind of novel in which good supporting characters are necessary, and Pendennis has much better support than Philip. The Victorians loved a crowded scene with active vivid characters and *Pendennis* takes its place as one of the great Victorian character collections.

The most engaging is the old soldier, Major Pendennis, the only sophisticated old soldier Thackeray has given us. The Major's handling of women and his management of Pen's calf-love affair are the essential joys of the novel. The sentimental feeling for the strolling players and Mr Bowes, and the harsh macabre Clavering characters provide piquant contrast. The Oxford scenes are not so good perhaps, for Thackeray went to the other place, but Foker is a jolly character and Warrington, the last of the Warringtons in Thackeray, carries about with him the family aura. Together, Foker and Warrington provide the necessary foils to the hero. It is a book without attractive women. Pen's mother is insipid, the Fotheringay is designed to be heavy on hand, Fanny Bolton is almost impossibly dim, and Blanche Amory is completely unattractive. Laura comes into her own later, as Mrs Pendennis. It is a weakness of the plot that most of these women *have* to be unattractive, but the compensation is that there is a wealth of London characters, since the apprenticeship of Pendennis is a long and varied experience.

As with people, so with places. *Pendennis* gives us Warrington and Captain Shandon, and it also gives us their backgrounds in the Middle Temple and the Fleet Prison. They are all drawn to give his readers glimpses of their own city which they would never see for themselves and many of them are recalled from Thackeray's own apprentice-

[1] So named from Goethe's novel *Wilhelm Meister's Apprenticeship*.

ship, his apparently wasted youth. It is the world of *The Book of Snobs* and other earlier papers, presented with much less obvious ridicule and with what seems to us an excess of sentiment.

There is the same leaning towards sentiment in *The Newcomes*, which Thackeray built out of another part of his mental store, his recollections of his Anglo-Indian relations. Once again there is a splendid sufficiency of London sketches. The Cave of Harmony, the chambers in the Temple, the studios of the young painters, the dinners in the Squares. Once again there is a world of characters, the like of which the suburbs and posterity would never otherwise have known. Professional writers, Pendennis and Bayham; aristocrats, Kew and Jack Belsize; Anglo-Indians, the Colonel himself and the civilian, James Binnie; a fashionable preacher, Mr Honeyman, with his Jewish backer, who promotes the parson as he would any other profitable performer. It is a book in which the minor characters are sharp in recollection, firm, gritty, real. They hold the interest, from James Binnie and the sweet Miss Honeyman to the Campaigner.

The two outstanding characters are the Colonel and Ethel. Both are studies of goodness, and characters with this quality are not only difficult to make interesting, they are difficult to make at all. Fairly early in the story, Thackeray found himself in difficulties over the Colonel and packed him off back to India. Later, he returns to be the foil to his banker relations, who typify the general closeness of the Victorian money world. The Colonel goes into their banking world, fails egregiously and retains his integrity and his goodness. Thackeray loved these retired soldiers, so like his step-father, who had an eccentricity based on native gentleness and an atrabilious fieriness nourished under the Indian sun.

Before the crash, Colonel Newcome is a fighting champion for the young people. When Barnes Newcome tells lies to keep Ethel and Clive apart 'the cup of Thomas Newcome's wrath overflowed. Barnes had lied about Ethel's visit to

London; Barnes had lied in saying that he delivered the message with which his uncle charged him; Barnes had lied about the letter which he had received, and never sent. With these accusations firmly proven in his mind against his nephew, the Colonel went down to confront that sinner.' He found him in his bank:

'This young gentleman is one of your clerks?' asked Thomas Newcome, blandly.

'Yes: Mr Boltby, who has your private account. This is Colonel Newcome, Mr Boltby', says Sir Barnes, in some wonder.

'Mr Boltby, brother Hobson, you heard what Sir Barnes Newcome said just now respecting certain intelligence, which he grieved to give me?'

At this all three gentlemen respectively wore looks of amazement.

'Allow me to say in your presence, that I don't believe one single word Sir Barnes Newcome says, when he tells me that he is very sorry for some intelligence he has to communicate. He lies, Mr Boltby; he is very glad. I made up my mind that in whatsoever company I met him, and on the very first day I found him—hold your tongue, sir; you shall speak afterwards and tell more lies when I have done—I made up my mind, I say, that on the very first occasion I would tell Sir Barnes Newcome that he was a liar and a cheat. He takes charge of letters and keeps them back. Did you break the seal, sir? There was nothing to steal in my letter to Miss Newcome. He tells me people are out of town whom he goes to see in the next street, after leaving my table, and whom I see myself half an hour after he lies to me about their absence.'

'Damn you, go out, and don't stand staring there, you booby!' screams out Sir Barnes to the clerk. 'Stop, Boltby. Colonel Newcome, unless you leave this room I shall—I shall——'

'You shall call a policeman. Send for the gentleman, and I will tell the Lord Mayor what I think of Sir Barnes Newcome, Baronet. Mr Boltby, shall we have the constable in?'

'Sir, you are an old man, and my father's brother, or you know very well I would——'

'You would what, sir? Upon my word, Barnes Newcome' (here the Colonel's two hands and the bamboo cane came from the rear and formed in front), 'but that you are my father's grandson, after a menace like that, I would take you out and cane you in the presence of your clerks. I repeat, sir, that I consider you guilty of treachery, falsehood, and knavery. And if ever I see you at the Bay's Club, I will make the same statement to your acquaintance at the west end of the town. A man of your baseness ought to be known, sir; and it shall be my business to make men of honour aware of your character. Mr Boltby, will you have the kindness to make out my account? Sir Barnes Newcome, for fear of consequences which I shall deplore, I recommend you to keep a wide berth of me, sir.' And the Colonel twirled his mustachios, and waved his cane in an ominous manner, and Barnes started back spontaneously out of its dangerous circle.

But Thackeray is a realist and in the end the Colonel goes down and Barnes flourishes.

The Colonel is still more sympathetic in adversity. When he comes home to tell his family that he has lost all his money and is about to be declared bankrupt, the scene opens thus:

'Has it come, Father?' said Clive, with a sure prescience, looking in his father's face.

The father took and grasped the hand which his son held out. 'Let us go back into the dining-room', he said. They entered it, and he filled himself a glass of wine out of the bottle still standing amidst the dessert. He bade the butler retire, who was lingering about the room and sideboard, and only wanted to know whether his master would have dinner, that was all. And, this gentleman having withdrawn, Colonel Newcome finished his glass of sherry and broke a biscuit; the Campaigner assuming an attitude of surprise and indignation, whilst Rosey had leisure to remark that Papa looked very ill, and that something must have happened.

The vulgar outcries of the two women follow and when they have gone, the scene ends thus:

'Here's a good end to it', says Clive, with flashing eyes and a flushed face, 'and here's a health till to-morrow, Father!' and he filled into two glasses the wine still remaining in the flask. 'Goodbye to our fortune, and bad luck go with her—I puff the prostitute away—*Si celeres quatit pennas*, you remember what we used to say at Grey Friars—*resigno quae dedit, et mea virtute me involve, probamque pauperiem sine dote quaero.*' And he pledged his father, who drank his wine, his hand shaking as he raised the glass to his lips, and his kind voice trembling as he uttered the well-known old school words, with an emotion that was as sacred as a prayer. Once more, and with hearts full of love, the two men embraced.

They fell back instinctively on their training and behaved well. This is a glimpse of the generations which Thackeray loved to give, the other side of the Victorian medal from *Father and Son* and *The Way of All Flesh*. It is on a par with Philip's loyalty to his father. It is the pristine brightness of family honour preserved in the actions and demeanour of the young.

In Ethel, Thackeray had his greatest success in portraying a heroine. Her character developed in opposition to the mercenary outlook of her family. She is a portrait of a natural aristrocrat; she is all that the upper middle classes could have wished to be. We feel that she is the counterpart of the Colonel, and that when she at last marries Clive (we hear casually in *Philip* that they did marry) she will make as fine a man of him as his father was. Goodness is a quality that is apt to turn into something else while it is being described. Thackeray overcame the difficulty simply. He presents Ethel to us by the simple means of letting us see her through other eyes. For example, through the eyes of Laura Pendennis, whose judgement on women we trust as much as Pendennis did himself. Or through the eyes of Pendennis and the old family solicitor in this typical Victorian novel scene of joy and salvation through splendid generosity with money. Ethel has discovered that a great part of the money she has inherited should have gone to Clive in justice though not in law. Without hesitation she demands of her brother Barnes that her grandmother's wish be honoured. They quarrel because he refuses, and she asks Pendennis to take her to the family solicitor. It is her nature not to rest until the thing is put right:

'. . . I consulted with this gentleman, the husband of my dearest friend, Mrs Pendennis—the most intimate friend of my uncle and cousin Clive; and I wish, and I desire and insist, that my share of what my poor father left us girls should be given to my cousin, Mr Clive Newcome, in accordance with my grandmother's dying wishes.'

'My dear, you gave away your portion to your brothers and sisters ever so long ago!' cried the lawyer.

'I desire, sir, that six thousand pounds may be given to my cousin', Miss Newcome said, blushing deeply. 'My dear uncle, the best man in the world, whom I love with all my heart, sir, is in the most dreadful poverty. Do you know where he is, sir? My dear, kind, generous uncle!' —and, kindling as she spoke, and with eyes beaming a bright kindness, and flushing cheeks, and a voice that thrilled to the heart of those two who heard her, Miss Newcome went on to tell of her uncle's and cousin's misfortunes, and of her wish, under God, to relieve them. I see before me now the figure of the noble girl as she speaks; the pleased little lawyer, bobbing his white head, looking up at her with his twinkling eyes—patting his knees, patting his snuff-box—as he sits before his tapes and his deeds, surrounded by a great background of tin boxes.

'And I understand you want this money paid as coming from the family, and not from Miss Newcome?' says Mr Luce.

'Coming from the family—exactly'—answers Miss Newcome.

Mr Luce rose up from his old chair—his worn-out old horsehair chair—where he had sat for half a century and listened to many a speaker very different from this one. 'Mr Pendennis', he said, 'I envy you your journey along with this young lady. I envy you the good news you are going to carry to your friends—and, Miss Newcome, as I am an old—old gentleman who has known your family these sixty years, and saw your father in his long-clothes, may I tell you how heartily and sincerely I—I love and respect you, my dear? When should you wish Mr Newcome to have his legacy?'

'I think I should like Mr Pendennis to have it this instant, Mr Luce, please', said the young lady.

These two characters, Ethel and the Colonel, stand out, and the scenes in which they appear stand out in a general level of performance which is too relaxed to be as uniformly amusing as *Pendennis*. There is just a thought at times that for lack of interest in the characters he has got on his hands, Thackeray calls up a world of new ones to see if they are any more amusing. He is competent always; he is always dexterous, and whenever necessary he displays the virtuosity of the professional performer. In the end, there can be no quarrelling with a novel that gives us characters like Ethel and Colonel Newcome and old Lady Kew, or scenes like the old Anglo-Indians' dinner party in Clifford Street,

Mr Honeyman preaching, the studios of the young artists and the auctioning of all the Colonel's splendour. There are moments in *The Newcomes* which we remember as we remember all moments of especially percipient understanding. One of them is when young Lord Kew releases Ethel after she has shown him the letter:

> When he saw Ethel again, which he did in an hour's time, the generous young gentleman held his hand out to her. 'My dear', he said, 'if you had loved me you never would have shown me that letter.' It was his only reproof. After that he never again reproved or advised her.

He knew whom Ethel loved, but we are no more sure than in real life whether Ethel knew herself. Not many novelists have that quality of realism, and our enjoyment of the English novel is incomplete if we have missed *The Newcomes*.

Of the trilogy which forms the Pendennis sequence, *Philip* is the weakest; but its reputation is much lower than it deserves, probably because of the very poor opening chapters. Thackeray had long been unwell, and when he took over the *Cornhill* in 1860, he had hoped to have *Philip* ready for serial use. When it came to the point he only had that strange performance, *Lovel the Widower*, and had to coax Anthony Trollope to fill the place of *Philip* with *Framley Parsonage*.

The interest of *Philip*, after the slow, weak opening, is that it is a development of the Pendennis autobiographical disclosures. The old man is commenting freely and sadly on his own youth. It is a classical *locus* in the English novel of our wincing memories of youthful incidents. Later on it takes us right back to *The Great Hoggarty Diamond* in being a celebration of young love and early married life.

Thackeray never made a gentler hero nor one who suffered so much. Philip's nerves are jangling all the time and the narrator at times is hardly in better case. At moments it almost seems that too much watching of this London Vanity Fair was driving the observer mad. 'The atmosphere of those polite drawing-rooms stifles me. I can't bow the knee to the horrible old Mammon. I walk about in the crowds as lonely as if I was in a wilderness. . .' It is Philip, not Pendennis, speaking there but it is also Thackeray. Philip's nostalgic gentleness saves him, just as it helps him to endure his father.

Philip in this matter is a precursor of the later Victorian pictures of unhappy father-son relationships, by Samuel Butler and Edmund Gosse. But the psychology is different. Philip begins as an Angry Young Man, but he rapidly develops and becomes generous, and nothing that his father does can embitter the gentleness of his spirit.

The novel begins weakly and for three chapters is grey and thin. Suddenly, in Chapter Four, the old Thackeray virtuosity reappears, and the diffuse, entrancing monologue is on. Love at first sight in Boulogne, the quarrel of the old officers in the dreary *pension* in Paris, the narrator's own domestic background and the fury of the mother-in-law. Have these things been bettered in Thackeray or elsewhere? We are ready to enjoy the paintings of Frith these days, and we adore a crinoline. The whole Victorian age, mahogany by gaslight, is engaging our willing attention. Shall we continue to neglect these Pendennis novels which offers us the most subtle imaginative prose writing of the 'fifties?

The pleasures we find there are the pleasures that we value in life; humour and urbanity, based on security. For behind the personal misfortunes which make the plots is a perfectly secure social structure moving with glacial slowness towards inevitable betterment.

VII.   *CORNHILL* AND THE LECTURES

Thackeray was a bad editor. He was too kind, and the office work bored him. But his name gave *Cornhill* an immense impetus, so that it started with the phenomenal sale of

110,000, which shows what an avid public the publishers had made in London during Thackeray's lifetime. Thackeray's personal contribution was first of all the second serial, *Lovel the Widower*, and then *Philip*. After his death there was *Denis Duval*, but far better than any of these were the *Roundabout Papers*, in which he exploited so well those gifts as an essayist which are indicated in the Pendennis books.

Lovel the Widower is a pale performance, but it has quite exceptional interest for the student of Thackeray. Everyone in the story is improbable and so are the incidents. The story line is similar to the one used in so many early Thackeray long-short stories, a gentle build-up to a final dramatic scene. The special interest is the heroine. In her we see Thackeray going as far as he dare in faithfully showing the nature of a strongly-sexed woman. She is a governess in a widower's family in an expensive Putney household. She has that fatal attraction which affects all the men around her, the butler, the apothecary, the narrator and her master. Needless to say, she chooses her master, who unexpectedly declares himself in the classic comic situation, when she is just going to be sent packing by his mother and mother-in-law. This is a curious counterpart of the normal satirizing of the Victorian marriage market. Never does he show such heartless calculation as in this girl who looks after herself without a moment's thought for any of her victims. The story line is a powerful one, but the actual telling is weak. The reader feels, as in the opening of *Philip*, that the writer is ill, and the performance lacks stereoscopic reality.

If the late novels were a sort of confidential talk, the lectures were all that was formal in public speaking. Thackeray went out lecturing because he wanted to leave plenty of money to his two daughters. Dickens had been wonderfully successful with his readings, why should Thackeray not cash in on the popular desire in Britain and America to see and hear the popular writer?

He prepared *The English Humourists* first. They have very little value to the student today though Thackeray made no mistake about who were the best eighteenth-century writers. But his view on the eighteenth century and ours are poles apart, and if his lectures are read with appreciation at all today it will be by the professional lecturer. They are a model for the presentation of a literary subject to a philistine audience. He knew that he had to presume complete ignorance. He began with Swift, and quoted Swift for comparison when he came to Steele, and both when he came to Addison and so on, comparing and at the same time reminding.

His method is to tell the story of these writers' lives and to draw their characters. The common reader loves it, as Somerset Maugham has shown us in our own time. By using this technique, Thackeray was able to quote from his authors without alarming his audience. It was an ideal way of giving a popular audience as much as it could comfortably digest. When it came to printing them, he extended the anthology in the text by adding copious quotations as footnotes. Simple and agreeable, but today these lectures are only interesting for what they tell us about the lecturer.

The Four Georges were prepared originally for American consumption and in them he develops a point of view in courteous deference to his audience. His views are those with which we are familiar in *Barry Lyndon* and *The Virginians*. None of these lectures is much read now, although they enjoyed a long success in book form. They certainly cannot be recommended to students of the eighteenth century.

By contrast, the *Roundabout Papers* are still excellent reading. In the great days of their mature reputations, both Dickens and Thackeray had forums from which they could speak to their readers. Dickens wrote *The Uncommercial Traveller* in *All the Year Round* and Thackeray the *Roundabout Papers* in *Cornhill*. Each took the opportunity in these periodical essays of writing an occasional lay sermon.

Dickens produced some savagely true and stern denunciations of Victorian life, while Thackeray's mood was different. He fought the evil that he saw through compassion. In an essay called *On a Chalk-mark on the Door* he talks about the servants, the people whose lives had haunted him ever since his first writings in the *Yellowplush* papers. Here, we have the nearest Thackeray got to the shame Victorians felt about the two nations in England:

> I am not going into the horrid old question of 'followers', I don't mean cousins from the country, love-stricken policemen, or gentlemen in mufti from Knightsbridge Barracks; but people who have an occult right on the premises; the uncovenanted servants of the house; grey women who are seen at evening, with baskets flitting about area-railings; dingy shawls which drop you furtive curtseys in your neighbourhood; demure little Jacks who start up from behind boxes in the pantry. Those outsiders wear Thomas's crest and livery, and call him 'Sir'; those silent women address the female servants as 'Mum', and curtsey before them, squaring their arms over their wretched lean aprons. Then, again, those *servi servorum* have dependants in the vast, silent, poverty-stricken world outside your comfortable kitchen fire, in the world of darkness, and hunger, and miserable cold, and dank flagged cellars, and huddled straw, and rags, in which pale children are swarming.

In another Roundabout paper he sums up all his attempts and desires as a writer. Here is the spirit behind *Barry Lyndon* and *Henry Esmond* and *Denis Duval*, and the spirit behind the Pendennis books: 'If the gods would give me the desire of my heart, I should be able to write a story which boys would relish for the next few dozen centuries. The boy-critic loves the story: grown up, he loves the author who wrote the story.' Could there be a neater explanation of the Thackeray *œuvre*? Or a prouder mock repentance than this? '. . . perhaps of all the novel-spinners now extant, the present speaker is the most addicted to preaching. Does he not stop perpetually in his story and begin to preach to you? . . . I cry *peccavi* loudly and heartily.' Whatever we may feel about the preaching in the novels, we all enjoy these *Roundabout Papers* and each of us can name his favourites. The Victorians, when we come to think of it, were not usually intimate writers. Anyone who wishes to meet intimately one of the finest Victorian minds could hardly do better than read the *Roundabout Papers*.

VIII. CONCLUSION

If a writer produces an *œuvre*, he may be expected to produce a point of view. Thackeray, the realist, the satirist, the commentator, could not fail to do so. But his point of view as shown in his fiction is limited and confined. He lived and worked through the worst of the Industrial Revolution. During his lifetime space and time were being contracted in England by the railways. The troubles of the north came more quickly south. He lived through the Oxford Movement and the scientific revolution marked usually by *The Origin of Species*. His great decade was also the decade of the Crimean War and the Indian Mutiny. We search his writings in vain for any mention of these things. Not that there was any social inhibition about any of these subjects. There were novelists then as now who could not escape being involved, men like Disraeli and Kingsley. But Thackeray, concerned with the secular problems, did not trouble to focus contemporary events.

He honoured his contract as a novelist by writing of personal and family relationships with a highly developed historical sense. The reader feels not only that he is following the fortunes of the Esmonds and Warringtons through the generations, but watching how each generation honoured its responsibilities towards society and passed them on to the next. It is this quality in the Thackeray panorama which gives it moral quality and depth.

There is nothing of this in the early brilliance of the Regency short novels. There is very little of it in *Barry Lyndon*, which is a mature work in giving us a sense of the unity of western Europe. It is first developed in *Vanity Fair*, and the success of *Vanity Fair* gave him hope. But very soon he was cribbed, cabined and confined by the conventions of his age. He published *Pendennis*, and as soon as it was completed he commented in the preface:

> Since the author of *Tom Jones* was buried, no writer of fiction among us has been permitted to depict to his utmost power a MAN. We must drape him, and give him a certain conventional simper. Society will not tolerate the Natural in our Art.

In his next book, *Esmond*, he tried history again, offering a maturity and breadth of judgement which is only surpassed by the now neglected Scott. Both *Esmond* and *The Virginians* give a picture of a responsible society with values which were those out of which the values of Thackeray's own upper middle class had developed. For Esmond, Wolfe and Lambert are the men we are invited to admire, and whose like we long for in the leadership of the nation. Since *Esmond* was a comparative failure with his public, he returned in *The Newcomes* and *Philip*, as a professional writer must, to what his public expected of him. He gave up the splendours of moral judgement on great historical scenes and figures. He returned to the domestic scene, with the snob appeal of the upper middle classes and the spice of satire. He did what he was allowed to do, he criticized society within the conventions of his public. Since his greatest work is written near the 'fifties or in them, the golden decade of the English upper middle classes to which he belonged, his 'criticism' may be expected to be a celebration of the virtues that class most reverenced.

It is in fact so. In *Vanity Fair*, it is virtue and generosity of spirit which are shown to be most potent. In the context of *Vanity Fair*, where the characters pursue their selfish ends, the human condition is shown to be man at the mercy of his desires, and society a compact of mutually tolerated selfishness; sudden uncalculated moments of generosity or blazing virtue change the course of the story. These generous moments are paid for in *Vanity Fair*, but they have the power that goes with truth and generous thought and action.

Thackeray goes further back, into his beloved eighteenth century, to give us characters of steady, unfaltering virtue, who form that core of society which carries it forward. Not the establishment, which is a compromise with the way of the world, the grand committee of top people in Vanity Fair, but the individual virtuous man, celebrated in European thinking by the Romans and always since. In Thackeray, men like Colonel Esmond and Colonel Lambert. They are men of integrity and quality who never compromise with evil.

These men were in no sense in opposition, they were apart. Opposition in Thackeray, opposition being that stress in human society which keeps it vital, is between the middle and lower classes. And the lower classes in Thackeray's novels are the servants. In their own way, they criticize and influence; they are always there, observing. Of the vast army of mechanics and labourers who followed Methodism and Charles Dickens, Thackeray knows nothing. It is all completely outside his imaginative world.

But from the beginning, he is intensely conscious of this opposition in society. The *Yellowplush* papers show it and it is present in *Vanity Fair* and *Pendennis*, Indeed, the nearest thing to social revolution and chaos in Thackeray is the revolt of Major Pendennis's man and the occupation of the Rawdon's flat by the servants who own it. In Thackeray's almost impregnable middle-class society, that is the only crack. A servant becoming rich by exploiting his careless master and using the power of his wealth in a vulgar way.

In that great portrait of an age, the Pendennis novels, we have Thackeray's mature and settled view of the society which he observed. He has no doubts about its power and its quality. It will go on for ever; that is in the nature of things. It will be compact of evil, and there will be generous, lovely people who will suffer and often survive and sometimes prevail. Neither good nor evil is confined to any stratum of society and there is no more likelihood of finding virtue in one stratum than in another.

In *Denis Duval* comes the last word on these social questions. Evil destroys society. Virtue builds it and holds it together. That is completely commonplace; but when Thackeray adumbrates it in the texture of his mature narrative prose, it becomes moving and exciting again. Since Thackeray's time our views have been modified. We are no longer certain that the upper middle classes and their beliefs will go on for ever because they are in the nature of things. We are at that stage in a social revolution when nearly everything is in doubt. So it is the middle classes who now return to Thackeray; for he painted their portrait in their hey-day.

But for all of us, Thackeray, in the normal course of his business as a professional writer, provides the best portrait we have of the class that was ruling England a hundred years ago. He observes the human scene with amusement and with the regard of a complete man, with the full range between the sentimental and the satirical. Like so many of the great men in that brilliantly rich generation, he could look at the human condition without despair.

THACKERAY

A Select Bibliography

(Place of publication London, unless stated otherwise)

Bibliography:

WILLIAM MAKEPEACE THACKERAY, 2 vols, by 'Lewis Melville' (1910)
—an enumerative bibliography of 1,300 items is in Vol. II,
pp. 143-376.

A THACKERAY LIBRARY, by H. S. Van Duzer; New York (1919).

THACKERAY'S CRITICS. An Annotated Bibliography of British and
American Criticism, 1836-1901, edited with Introduction by
D. Flamm; Chapel Hill, North Carolina (1966).

Note: A full, definitive bibliography remains a desideratum. There are
important Thackeray collections, which have been catalogued, at
Princeton (Parrish Collection) and in the New York Public Library
(Berg Collection).

Collected Works:

MISCELLANIES: PROSE AND VERSE, 4 vols; Leipzig (Vol. I 1849; Vol. II
1851; Vol. III 1856; Vol. IV 1857)

—Vol. I contains *The Great Hoggarty Diamond, The Book of Snobs;*
Vol. II *The Kickleburys Abroad, Rebecca and Rowena*, etc.; Vols. III
and IV the contents of the London Miscellanies (see next entry)
apart from the above.

MISCELLANIES: PROSE AND VERSE, 4 vols (1855-7; reprinted 1861
and 1865)

—Vol. I includes *The Book of Snobs* and *Major Gahagan;* Vol. II *The
Memoirs of Mr Yellowplush, Novels by Eminent Hands;* Vol. III *The
Memoirs of Barry Lyndon, A Legend of the Rhine, Rebecca and Rowena;*
Vol. IV *The Fitz-Boodle Papers, A Shabby Genteel Story, The Great
Hoggarty Diamond.* The selection, made by Thackeray himself,
provides the most convenient introduction to his early writings.
For other collections of miscellaneous essays and stories, see the
Cambridge Bibliography of English Literature, III (1969), cols 856-859.

WORKS, 22 vols (1867-9; 24 vols 1885-6)

—the Library Edition.

WORKS, 26 vols (1878-86)

—with a Memoir by Sir L. Stephen.

WORKS, 17 vols (1908)

—the Oxford Edition. Introductions by G. Saintsbury. With original
and revised readings, and additional material.

WORKS, 26 vols (1910-11)

—the Centenary Edition, with biographical introductions by Anne Thackeray Ritchie. These are useful and are profusely embellished with Thackeray's drawings. Includes Sir L. Stephen's Memoir.

Note: There are other collected editions, notably those edited by H. E. Scudder (22 vols, Boston, 1889); edited by W. Jerrold (30 vols, 1901-3); edited by 'L. Melville' (20 vols 1901-7; 1911).

THE LETTERS AND PRIVATE PAPERS, collected and edited by G. N. Ray, 4 vols; Cambridge, Mass. (1946).

W. M. THACKERAY. Contributions to the 'Morning Chronicle' ed. G. N. Ray; Urbana (1955).

Separate Works:

THE PROFESSOR. A TALE (1837)
—first published in *Bentley's Miscellany*, 1837.

MEMOIRS OF MR C. J. YELLOWPLUSH [with] THE DIARY OF C. JEAMES DE LA PLUCHE, ESQR. (1856). *Comic pieces*
—first published in *Fraser's Magazine*, 1837-8, as *The Yellowplush Correspondence*.

SOME PASSAGES IN THE LIFE OF MAJOR GAHAGAN (1838-9). *Burlesque short novel*
—first published in the *New Monthly Magazine*, 1838-9.

CATHERINE, a story, by Ikey Solomons, Esq. (1839-40). *Short novel*
—first published in *Fraser's Magazine*, 1839-40.

STUBB'S CALENDAR; OR, THE FATAL BOOTS (1839). *Comic journalism*
—first published in *Cruikshank's Comic Annual*, 1839.

THE BEDFORD ROW CONSPIRACY (1840). *Short novel*
—first published in *New Monthly Magazine*, 1840.

THE PARIS SKETCH BOOK, by Mr Titmarsh, 2 vols (1840). *Prose sketches*

A SHABBY GENTEEL STORY; New York (1852). *Short novel*
—first published in *Fraser's Magazine*, 1840.

AN ESSAY ON THE GENIUS OF GEORGE CRUIKSHANK (1840). *Criticism*
—first published in the *Westminster Review*, 1840.

BARBER COX AND THE CUTTING OF HIS COMB (1840). *Comic journalism*
—first published in *Cruikshank's Comic Annual. Cox's Diaries* in the *Miscellanies*.

THE GREAT HOGGARTY DIAMOND; New York (1848). *Short novel*
—first published in *Fraser's Magazine*, 1841.

THE SECOND FUNERAL OF NAPOLEON . . . AND THE CHRONICLE OF THE DRUM (1841). *Historical essay.*

THE FITZ-BOODLE PAPERS (1852). *Comic journalism*
—first published in *Fraser's Magazine*, 1842-3.

MISS TICKLETOBY'S LECTURES ON ENGLISH HISTORY (1852). *Comic journalism*
—first published in *Punch*, 1842.

THE CONFESSIONS OF GEORGE FITZ-BOODLE (1843). *Comic journalism*
—first published in *Fraser's Magazine*, 1843. Reprinted with *The Fitz-Boodle Papers*, 1852 (see above).

THE IRISH SKETCH-BOOK, 2 vols by M. A. Titmarsh (1843). *Prose sketches*

BLUEBEARD'S GHOST, by M. A. Titmarsh (1843). *Short story*
—first published in *Fraser's Magazine*, 1843.

THE LUCK OF BARRY LYNDON. A ROMANCE OF THE LAST CENTURY, by Fitz-Boodle, 2 vols; New York (1852). *Novel*
—first published in *Fraser's Magazine*, 1844. Revised as *The Memoirs of Barry Lyndon, Esq.*, 1856.

A LEGEND OF THE RHINE, by Michael Angelo Titmarsh (1845). *Comic journalism*
—first published in *George Cruikshank's Table-Book*, 1845.

JEAMES'S DIARY; OR, SUDDEN WEALTH; New York (1846). *Comic journalism*
—first published in *Punch*, 1845-6, as *Jeames's Diary*.

PROPOSALS FOR A CONTINUATION OF 'IVANHOE' (1846). *Parody*
—first published in *Fraser's Magazine*. Revised as *Rowena and Rebecca*, 1850 (see below).

NOTES OF A JOURNEY FROM CORNHILL TO GRAND CAIRO . . . , by M. A. Titmarsh (1846). *Travel*

THE BOOK OF SNOBS (incomplete 1848; complete, New York, 1852). *Satire*
—first published in *Punch*, 1846-7, as *The Snobs of England*.

VANITY FAIR. A NOVEL WITHOUT A HERO (1847-8). *Novel*
—first published in 20 monthly parts, January 1847-July 1848. Edited by G. and K. Tillotson, 1963.

MRS PERKINS'S BALL, by M. A. Titmarsh (1847). *Short novel*

A LITTLE DINNER AT TIMMINS'S (1848). *Short novel*
—first published in *Punch*, 1848.

'OUR STREET' by Mr M. A. Titmarsh (1848). *Short novel*

THE HISTORY OF PENDENNIS. HIS FORTUNES AND MISFORTUNES, HIS
FRIENDS AND HIS GREATEST ENEMY, 2 vols (1849-50). *Novel*
—first published in 24 monthly parts, November 1848-December
1850.

DOCTOR BIRCH AND HIS YOUNG FRIENDS, by Mr M. A. Titmarsh (1849).
Short novel.

REBECCA AND ROWENA. A ROMANCE UPON ROMANCE, by Mr M. A.
Titmarsh (1850). *Parody*

THE KICKLEBURYS ON THE RHINE, by Mr M. A. Titmarsh (1850). *Short
novel*

THE HISTORY OF HENRY ESMOND, ESQRE. A COLONEL IN THE SERVICE OF
HER MAJESTY Q. ANNE, written by himself, 3 vols (1852). *Novel*
—edited by G. N. Ray, New York, 1950.

THE ENGLISH HUMOURISTS OF THE EIGHTEENTH CENTURY (1853). *Lectures*
—a series delivered in Great Britain and the USA.

THE NEWCOMES. MEMOIRS OF A MOST RESPECTABLE FAMILY. Edited by
Arthur Pendennis, Esqre., 2 vols (1854-5; revised 1863). *Novel*
—first published in 24 monthly parts, October 1853-August 1855.

BALLADS (1855).

THE ROSE AND THE RING: OR, THE HISTORY OF PRINCE GIGLIO AND PRINCE
BULBO. A FIRESIDE PANTOMIME FOR GREAT AND SMALL CHILDREN, by
Mr M. A. Titmarsh (1855)
—a fascimile (ed. G. N. Ray) of the original manuscript in the
Morgan Library was published in New York, 1947.

THE VIRGINIANS. A TALE OF THE LAST CENTURY, 2 vols (1858-9). *Novel*
—first published in 24 monthly parts, November 1857-September
1859.

LOVEL THE WIDOWER (1861). *Novel*
—first published in the *Cornhill Magazine*, 1860.

THE FOUR GEORGES: SKETCHES OF MANNERS, MORALS, COURT AND TOWN
LIFE; New York (1860), London (1861). *Lectures*

ROUNDABOUT PAPERS (1863). *Essays*
—first published in the *Cornhill Magazine*, 1860-3.

THE ADVENTURES OF PHILIP ON HIS WAY THROUGH THE WORLD, 3 vols
(1862). *Novel*
—first published in the *Cornhill Magazine*, 1861-2.

DENIS DUVAL; New York (1864), London (1867). *Novel*
—first published in the *Cornhill Magazine*, 1864. Published posthumously.

Some Biographical and Critical Studies:

THACKERAY IN THE UNITED STATES 1852-3, 1855-6, by J. G. Wilson;
2 vols (1904).

'Charles Dickens', by W. Bagehot, *National Review*, October 1858
—variously reprinted in book form. Probably the earliest of many
comparisons between Dickens and Thackeray.

'Sterne and Thackeray', by W. Bagehot, *National Review*, April 1864
—appears in *Literary Studies*, ed. R. H. Hutton, Vol. II, and in his
Works, ed. R. Barrington, Vol. IV, 1915.

THACKERAY, by A. Trollope (1879)
—in the English Men of Letters series. Almost as useful on Thackeray
as it is on Trollope.

W. M. THACKERAY, by C. Whibley (1903)
—sensitive, but marks the beginning of the critical revolt.

DICKENS AND THACKERAY, by O. Elton (1924).

CHARLES DICKENS AND OTHER VICTORIANS, by Sir A. Quiller-Couch;
Cambridge (1925).

A CONSIDERATION OF THACKERAY, by G. Saintsbury; Oxford (1931)
—a reprint in book form of the Introductions to the Oxford Edition of
The Works.

THACKERAY. A PERSONALITY, by M. Elwin (1932).

THACKERAY. L'HOMME, LE PENSEUR, LE ROMANCIER, by R. Las Vergnas;
Paris (1932).

THACKERAY, by G. U. Ellis (1933).

EARLY VICTORIAN NOVELISTS, by Lord D. Cecil (1934).

THACKERAY. A CRITICAL PORTRAIT, by J. W. Dodds; New York (1941).

THACKERAY. A RECONSIDERATION, by J. Y. T. Greig; Oxford (1950).

LAST ESSAYS, by G. M. Young (1950)
—contains a discerning review of the *Collected Letters*.

THACKERAY'S DAUGHTER: SOME RECOLLECTIONS OF ANNE THACKERAY,
compiled by H. F. Fuller and V. Hammersley; Dublin (1951).

THE BURIED LIFE, by G. N. Ray (1952)
—a useful short study of the novels, suggesting originals for many
of the characters.

THACKERAY THE NOVELIST, by G. Tillotson (1954)
—a valuable study. The many quotations are well chosen to show
Thackeray's quality as a stylist.

NOVELISTS OF THE EIGHTEEN-FORTIES, by K. Tillotson; Oxford (1954)
—invaluable on *Vanity Fair*.

THACKERAY. THE USES OF ADVERSITY, by G.N. Ray; London and New York (1955).

THACKERAY. THE AGE OF WISDOM, by G. N. Ray; London and New York (1958)
—the standard biography, authorized by the Thackeray family. The first volume carries the story up to *Vanity Fair;* the second completes it.

THACKERAY AND THE FORM OF FICTION, by J. Loofbourow; Princeton (1964).

WRITERS AND THEIR WORK

General Surveys:

THE DETECTIVE STORY IN BRITAIN:
Julian Symons

THE ENGLISH BIBLE: Donald Coggan

ENGLISH VERSE EPIGRAM:
G. Rostrevor Hamilton

ENGLISH HYMNS: A. Pollard

ENGLISH MARITIME WRITING:
Hakluyt to Cook: Oliver Warner

THE ENGLISH SHORT STORY I: & II:
T. O. Beachcroft

THE ENGLISH SONNET: P. Cruttwell

ENGLISH SERMONS: Arthur Pollard

ENGLISH TRAVELLERS IN THE
NEAR EAST: Robin Fedden

THREE WOMEN DIARISTS: M. Willy

Sixteenth Century and Earlier:

FRANCIS BACON: J. Max Patrick

BEAUMONT & FLETCHER: Ian Fletcher

CHAUCER: Nevill Coghill

GOWER & LYDGATE: Derek Pearsall

RICHARD HOOKER: A. Pollard

THOMAS KYD: Philip Edwards

LANGLAND: Nevill Coghill

LYLY & PEELE: G. K. Hunter

MALORY: M. C. Bradbrook

MARLOWE: Philip Henderson

SIR THOMAS MORE: E. E. Reynolds

RALEGH: Agnes Latham

SIDNEY: Kenneth Muir

SKELTON: Peter Green

SPENSER: Rosemary Freeman

THREE 14TH-CENTURY ENGLISH
MYSTICS: Phyllis Hodgson

TWO SCOTS CHAUCERIANS:
H. Harvey Wood

WYATT: Sergio Baldi

Seventeenth Century:

SIR THOMAS BROWNE: Peter Green

BUNYAN: Henri Talon

CAVALIER POETS: Robin Skelton

CONGREVE: Bonamy Dobrée

DONNE: F. Kermode

DRYDEN: Bonamy Dobrée

ENGLISH DIARISTS:
Evelyn and Pepys: M. Willy

FARQUHAR: A. J. Farmer

JOHN FORD: Clifford Leech

GEORGE HERBERT: T. S. Eliot

HERRICK: John Press

HOBBES: T. E. Jessop

BEN JONSON: J. B. Bamborough

LOCKE: Maurice Cranston

ANDREW MARVELL: John Press

MILTON: E. M. W. Tillyard

RESTORATION COURT POETS:
V. de S. Pinto

SHAKESPEARE: C. J. Sisson
  CHRONICLES: Clifford Leech
  EARLY COMEDIES: Derek Traversi
  LATER COMEDIES: G. K. Hunter
  FINAL PLAYS: F. Kermode
  HISTORIES: L. C. Knights
  POEMS: F. T. Prince
  PROBLEM PLAYS: Peter Ure
  ROMAN PLAYS: T. J. B. Spencer
  GREAT TRAGEDIES: Kenneth Muir

THREE METAPHYSICAL POETS:
Margaret Willy

WEBSTER: Ian Scott-Kilvert

WYCHERLEY: P. F. Vernon

Eighteenth Century:

BERKELEY: T. E. Jessop

BLAKE: Kathleen Raine

BOSWELL: P. A. W. Collins

BURKE: T. E. Utley

BURNS: David Daiches

WM. COLLINS: Oswald Doughty

COWPER: N. Nicholson

CRABBE: R. L. Brett

DEFOE: J. R. Sutherland

FIELDING: John Butt

GAY: Oliver Warner

GIBBON: C. V. Wedgwood

GOLDSMITH: A. Norman Jeffares

GRAY: R. W. Ketton-Cremer

HUME: Montgomery Belgion

JOHNSON: S. C. Roberts

POPE: Ian Jack

RICHARDSON: R. F. Brissenden

SHERIDAN: W. A. Darlington

CHRISTOPHER SMART: G. Grigson

SMOLLETT: Laurence Brander

STEELE, ADDISON: A. R. Humphreys

STERNE: D. W. Jefferson

SWIFT: J. Middleton Murry

SIR JOHN VANBRUGH: Bernard Harris

HORACE WALPOLE: Hugh Honour

Nineteenth Century:

MATTHEW ARNOLD: Kenneth Allott

JANE AUSTEN: S. Townsend Warner

BAGEHOT: N. St John-Stevas

THE BRONTË SISTERS: P. Bentley

BROWNING: John Bryson

E. B. BROWNING: Alethea Hayter

SAMUEL BUTLER: G. D. H. Cole

BYRON: Herbert Read

CARLYLE: David Gascoyne

LEWIS CARROLL: Derek Hudson
CLOUGH: Isobel Armstrong
COLERIDGE: Kathleen Raine
CREEVEY & GREVILLE: J. Richardson
DE QUINCEY: Hugh Sykes Davies
DICKENS: K. J. Fielding
  EARLY NOVELS: T. Blount
  LATER NOVELS: B. Hardy
DISRAELI: Paul Bloomfield
GEORGE ELIOT: Lettice Cooper
FERRIER & GALT: W. M. Parker
FITZGERALD: Joanna Richardson
MRS GASKELL: Miriam Allott
GISSING: A. C. Ward
THOMAS HARDY: R. A. Scott-James
                and C. Day Lewis
HAZLITT: J. B. Priestley
HOOD: Laurence Brander
G. M. HOPKINS: Geoffrey Grigson
T. H. HUXLEY: William Irvine
KEATS: Edmund Blunden
LAMB: Edmund Blunden
LANDOR: G. Rostrevor Hamilton
EDWARD LEAR: Joanna Richardson
MACAULAY: G. R. Potter
MEREDITH: Phyllis Bartlett
JOHN STUART MILL: M. Cranston
WILLIAM MORRIS: P. Henderson
NEWMAN: J. M. Cameron
PATER: Iain Fletcher
PEACOCK: J. I. M. Stewart
ROSSETTI: Oswald Doughty
CHRISTINA ROSSETTI: G. Battiscombe
RUSKIN: Peter Quennell
SIR WALTER SCOTT: Ian Jack
SHELLEY: G. M. Matthews
SOUTHEY: Geoffrey Carnall
R. L. STEVENSON: G. B. Stern
SWINBURNE: H. J. C. Grierson
TENNYSON: F. L. Lucas
THACKERAY: Laurence Brander
FRANCIS THOMPSON: P. Butter
TROLLOPE: Hugh Sykes Davies
OSCAR WILDE: James Laver
WORDSWORTH: Helen Darbishire

Twentieth Century:
CHINUA ACHEBE: A. Ravenscroft
W. H. AUDEN: Richard Hoggart
HILAIRE BELLOC: Renée Haynes
ARNOLD BENNETT: F. Swinnerton
EDMUND BLUNDEN: Alec M. Hardie
ELIZABETH BOWEN: Jocelyn Brooke
ROBERT BRIDGES: J. Sparrow
ROY CAMPBELL: David Wright
JOYCE CARY: Walter Allen
G. K. CHESTERTON: C. Hollis
WINSTON CHURCHILL: John Connell
R. G. COLLINGWOOD: E.W.F. Tomlin

I. COMPTON-BURNETT: P. H. Johnson
JOSEPH CONRAD: Oliver Warner
WALTER DE LA MARE: K. Hopkins
NORMAN DOUGLAS: Ian Greenlees
T. S. ELIOT: M. C. Bradbrook
FIRBANK & BETJEMAN: J. Brooke
FORD MADOX FORD: Kenneth Young
E. M. FORSTER: Rex Warner
CHRISTOPHER FRY: Derek Stanford
JOHN GALSWORTHY: R. H. Mottram
WM. GOLDING: Clive Pemberton
ROBERT GRAVES: M. Seymour-Smith
GRAHAM GREENE: Francis Wyndham
L. P. HARTLEY & ANTHONY POWELL:
        P. Bloomfield and B. Bergonzi
A. E. HOUSMAN: Ian Scott-Kilvert
ALDOUS HUXLEY: Jocelyn Brooke
HENRY JAMES: Michael Swan
PAMELA HANSFORD JOHNSON:
                Isabel Quigly
JAMES JOYCE: J. I. M. Stewart
RUDYARD KIPLING: Bonamy Dobrée
D. H. LAWRENCE: Kenneth Young
C. DAY LEWIS: Clifford Dyment
WYNDHAM LEWIS: E. W. F. Tomlin
COMPTON MACKENZIE: K. Young
LOUIS MACNEICE: John Press
KATHERINE MANSFIELD: Ian Gordon
JOHN MASEFIELD: L. A. G. Strong
SOMERSET MAUGHAM: J. Brophy
GEORGE MOORE: A. Norman Jeffares
EDWIN MUIR: J. C. Hall
J. MIDDLETON MURRY: Philip Mairet
SEAN O'CASEY: W. A. Armstrong
GEORGE ORWELL: Tom Hopkinson
JOHN OSBORNE: Simon Trussler
HAROLD PINTER: J. R. Taylor
POETS OF 1939-45 WAR: R. N. Currey
POWYS BROTHERS: R. C. Churchill
J. B. PRIESTLEY: Ivor Brown
HERBERT READ: Francis Berry
FOUR REALIST NOVELISTS: V. Brome
BERNARD SHAW: A. C. Ward
EDITH SITWELL: John Lehmann
OSBERT SITWELL: Roger Fulford
KENNETH SLESSOR: C. Semmler
C. P. SNOW: William Cooper
SYNGE & LADY GREGORY: E. Coxhead
DYLAN THOMAS: G. S. Fraser
G. M. TREVELYAN: J. H. Plumb
WAR POETS: 1914-18: E. Blunden
EVELYN WAUGH: Christopher Hollis
H. G. WELLS: Montgomery Belgion
PATRICK WHITE: R. F. Brissenden
ANGUS WILSON: K. W. Gransden
VIRGINIA WOOLF: B. Blackstone
W. B. YEATS: G. S. Fraser
ANDREW YOUNG & R. S. THOMAS:
                L. Clark and R. G. Thomas